Struggling for development

Struggling for
Development

Janis Berzins

LUXSIT

Published by
Lux Sit
Balasta dambis 70a-5
LV-1048, Riga, Latvia
info@luxsit.eu

Cover Image: Economic Worries by Petr Kratochvil.
CC0 1.0 Universal (CC0 1.0) license.

ISBN13: 978-9934-8396-4-1

Contents

For those trying to understand the world as it is
and not as it should be

Does the State Have a Role in Helping Latvia Exit this Crisis?

Jan 28, 2010

It is commonly believed that the Chinese word for "crisis" (Wei-Ji) is the combination of "danger" (Wei) with "opportunity" (Ji). Another interpretation is that the meaning of Ji in Wei-Ji is closer to the 'crucial point.' Whatever the correct meaning is, a time of crisis represents both ideas. It is a 'crucial point' in the sense that something is wrong and thus must be changed; at the same time it represents the opportunity to change things for the better. In other words, it is time to learn from past mistakes, to challenge current ideas, and to be open for learning different ones.

Two weeks ago there were two conferences in Riga discussing scenarios and possible solutions to Latvia's current crisis. Both stressed the necessity of the Latvian government having a more active role promoting economic development, instead of adopting policies that, in the words of the IMF, will result in "recession in the short run, and slow growth for several years to come." That is exactly what

Latvia cannot afford. Latvia needs to start acting now against the crisis.

The debate about the role of the state in promoting economic development so far has been mischaracterized. While there are two basic forms of state intervention, only one is usually mentioned: the one where the government regulates the economy so firmly that the private sector is penalized, leading to crisis. In short, the idea is that state intervention gives too much power to the labor unions, making real wages too high. In the beginning of the 1970s the result was falling global economic activity because of diminishing profits, together with inflation. While there is some truth to this narrative, it fails to mention the very important role played by the success of Keynesianism in promoting economic development.

However, there is another form of state intervention, where governments pursue development policies to help the private sector recover and flourish. In this case, there are a multitude of alternatives, from the now acceptable recipe of using a combination of developmental macroeconomic and fiscal policies, with nominal devaluation, to Asia's experience, where the government even established state-owned companies in sectors ignored by the private sector, as in chemicals, for example. This process is very well described in Ha-Joon Chang's book 'Bad Samaritans.' We do not have to go this far in Latvia, however, although a more ambitious plan focusing on effectively helping the private sector is necessary.

The first step has been done: state-owned Hipoteku Bank is finally being transformed into an investment bank, after ten years of discussions. If this was not imposed by the IMF, it is most likely that the Latvian civil servants and politicians would find excuses to postpone the process for many more years. There is an agreement signed with the European Investment Bank, for 100 million euros, to support the development of micro, small and medium enterprises and agricultural cooperative companies. This could be complemented by more discussion on how to further capitalize Hipoteku Bank, of which there are a number of possibilities.

Although the idea of micro and small enterprises as the main factor of economic development is currently very popular, it has some problems. Several studies have shown that they usually provide low value-added goods and services, besides having a short life. As a result, they may create as many jobs as they destroy. In developing countries such as Latvia, they are vulnerable to crisis cycles as the organizations are comparatively fragile. In other words, they are too volatile to promote economic development per se. They need to be part of a sector, functioning as part of a chain led by a bigger company. That's why a policy to promote economic development should focus on these complementarities. As a development bank, Hipoteku

Bank must have special programs to attract big investors to Latvia, to guarantee the proper level of economic dynamism to sustain the micro and small enterprises.

However, a development bank still may be not sufficient. First, the government must finally pass through administrative reform, not only to reduce the pressures on the budget, but also to be able to effectively deal with the necessities of the private sector, including the citizens. Second, it is urgent to reform the tax system to benefit business enterprises, ending the flat tax rate regime and introducing a progressive tax system for services such as real estate and financial market operations. For other services and for industry in general, a differentiated tax system is needed to help targeted sectors develop. For micro and small companies, a simplified accounting system is needed to cut costs. A temporary tax-free regime for new investors, including wage incentives, should be created.

Third, the government must establish industrial parks, with sufficient infrastructure, to attend to the concrete needs of the firms. Fourth, there should be professional schools to guarantee a sufficient supply of educated workers.

These policies are relatively easy to implement. Only the political will is necessary. Let's hope that Latvia's future development will not be jeopardized by a common lack of effort and understanding among politicians and authorities.

Oligarchs and Economic Development, or How to be a Failed State

Feb 25, 2010

Like other social sciences, economics is subject to an ideological cycle, subordinated to the appearance of crisis. Until the 1930s, classical liberalism based on laissez-faire was the main ideology determining economic policy; with the Great Depression, as a result of the failure of market determinism to deal with the huge level of unemployment at that time, Keynesianism turned to be the main economic ideology; with the process of stagflation experienced in the 1960s and 1970s, together with the oil shocks of 1973 and 1979, Keynesianism was substituted by a new ideology claiming to be the old liberalism with modern features, the self-proclaimed "neoliberalism."

This ideology's main feature is the strong helping belief that the State cannot interfere in the economy in any way, although, in practice, to helping financial institutions in trouble became a norm. When the Baltic States started the process of transition to capitalism, neoliberalism was the ideology in force, shaping what became known as "Shock Therapy." In other words, the economic model adopted by the Baltic States was based on the belief that the state has no role promoting economic development and market forces would always result in development, thus in full employment. After almost 20 years of transition, the fear of the leviathan state gave way to a permanent condition of state capture, where oligarchs manipulate or are politicians themselves, shape State institutions, and try to control the media to protect and advance their own empires at the expense of social and economic underdevelopment. Their names are widely known.

State capture may have several forms and levels, the most common being the directing of public contracts to specific companies, and the capture of institutions with regulatory power. This process artificially reproduces a situation similar to monopoly, where the outputs aren't optimal resulting in a social and economic dead-weight loss. Examples are airline companies or telecommunications providers capturing regulatory agencies in their favor, setting minimum tariffs at a higher level than what would be established by the market; construction firms influencing politicians to be awarded with contracts; companies using influence to reduce taxation.

In any case, although the results aren't the best for society, at least they guarantee high profit levels, usually resulting in more investments, thus in new jobs. In old capitalist countries, usually it is a process of indirect rent seeking: the actions are directed to increase corporate profits, which will result in bigger profits, salaries, and bonus. In the Baltic States, until now, this process occurred mainly through bogus privatizations, self-privatizations, pay-offs, and traffic of influence. In other words, State capture assumed the form of appropriation of state activities, like a large real estate business, to give jobs to family members, friends, and allies who usually are extremely incompetent to perform the activities they are expected to, and to make bidding to be directed to their own or their friends' and allies' companies. The point is that oligarchs, but also politicians and civil servants, see State capture as a way to private enrichment through the dilapidation of the State, and not to help business to be more profitable, even if the result is not economically optimal.

The problem is that the mentality of these people is still attached to the USSR's way of doing business, where the only way to have a normal life was to dilapidate the State to get personal gains. These people don't understand that they are very responsible for the poor level of economic development the Baltic Countries are experiencing. As discussed here some weeks ago, the State has an important role in promoting economic development. However, these people are impeding the State in doing that. Defending a pseudo free market ideology through their political influence, they impede the State in helping real business to flourish, while jeopardizing the State's capacity to do that.

When a parasite's victim dies, the parasite dies too. Time for these gentlemen to think about this.

Houdini and Immigration: Latvia's Solution for Economic Development

Mar 18, 2010

A very strong characteristic of the Baltic people is how they are united about preserving their cultural heritage, language, and society resulting in a specific form of nationalism. Immigration is a very sensitive part of this: more foreigners mean, proportionally, less indigenous people. As a result, the indigenous language, culture, and society are threatened. Most of Baltic politics have been subordinated to such sentiment. For example, why is there no metro in Riga? Because Latvians were against it. Facing low birth rates and years of all forms of ethnic cleansing by the Soviet Union, Latvians were worried that the immigration of workers from other parts of the Soviet Union could decrease even more their share in Latvia's social fabric. In 1988, a wave of protests with slogans like "No - metro, No - immigration," showed the real motives of the dissatisfaction among Latvians.

This month, immigration is again on spot. On March 13, President Valdis Zatlers returned to the Latvian

Parliament a polemic amendment on the Immigration Law. In summary, the amendment aims to ease foreign investors possibilities to obtain a temporary residence permit for up to 5 years. Thus, two kinds of investors are contemplated: (a) anyone investing 25,000 lats (35,700 euros) or more, employing at least 5 EU citizens, and paying no less than 10,000 lats in taxes; and (b) anyone with at least 100,000 lats to invest in real estate. Strangely, it has been presented as a real chance for Latvia to recover its economy. This idea is naive.

In the first case, the line of thought is simple: easier requirements for granting a residence permit will make foreign investors more interested in Latvia, boosting the amount of Foreign Direct Investment - FDI to Latvia. Unfortunately, a residence permit isn't the main determinant of FDI. Instead, economic theory and reality show that three main elements must be taken into consideration: (a) macro-economic stability (growth, inflation, exchange rate risk); (b) institutional stability (policies towards FDI, tax regimes, transparency of legal regulations, and level of corruption); and (c) political stability and level of democracy (political freedom, press freedom, liberty of expression). Latvia has tremendous problems in all these benchmarks, making this measure irrelevant.

The question of real estate is also problematic. The idea is that less bureaucratic requirements for investors to get a visa and enjoy their properties will boost the real estate market, thus Latvia's economy. There are two problems. First, this opens Latvia's and Schengen area's doors to any individual with money, representing a very serious threat to Europe's security. With Latvia's level of corruption, this is a very serious issue. Second, there is the economic question.

Although in the medium and long run investment in real estate is really a good option, very often what prevails is short-term speculation, with professionals in the field helping to fuel the illusion of easy money. Speculation with real estate, or 'easy money,' has a significant role in determining crises. The Great Depression of the 1930's, Sweden's and Finland's crises in the 1980's and 1990's, the Asian crisis, just to cite a few, were heavily influenced by speculation with real estate. The same applies to Latvia: speculation with real estate is one of the most important factors explaining the current depression. One important lesson in macroeconomics is that in a country, there is no place for 'easy money,' but for productive investments creating sustainable employment.

It is necessary to create an environment to help real business to flourish. It is time for politicians to understand that the only solution for Latvia's economic problems is the development of real and sustainable business, resulting from FDI. Although there is no magic in economics, just hard work to be done, politicians are still thinking they are Houdini here.

The opposition to this amendment is mainly based on nationalism against immigration. It should be different, as the problem is different. With the current economic crisis, the average Latvian is leaving the country trying to achieve a normal and dignified life. In practice, this has the same effect as immigration: there will be fewer Latvians in Latvia. Thus, it's necessary to find ways to stop emigration and to bring these people back. The key is economic development. Without Latvians, there is no Latvia. Latvian culture and language survived Swedes, Poles, Germans, and Russians. It seems they will not survive Latvian politicians and criminals self-labeled as 'honest' businessmen.

The Euro and its Crisis: a Financial or Structural Question?

Apr 22, 2010

Capitalism is constantly developing and advancing, resulting in qualitative changes in the way it reproduces itself. If until the 1970s, in both liberal and Keynesian capitalisms, the real sector (non-financial services and production of goods) was the most important to guarantee economic growth and development, since then the financial system has been assuming this role. This can be truly perceived by the rhetoric of the authorities, which care more about rating agencies and financial investments than about foreign direct investment in productive sectors. They forget that it is the latter that results in economic development. Thus, it seems that politicians and economists are forgetting about the real sector. This applies very much to the recent euro crisis.

Greece's fiscal deficit resulted in a wave of speculation against the euro, menacing other countries with bad financial health, like Spain, Portugal, Ireland, and Italy. As a result, for the first time, Eurozone countries promised to help one another that are in trouble. In this case Greece is cutting its deficits, but the financial markets do not understand the message, that the Eurozone countries would be ready to guarantee the block's stability and to help Athens. However, the problem is deeper and not directly related to financial markets. The main problem is the decentralization between monetary policy, conducted by the European Central Bank, and the instruments of economic policy (fiscal policy, wage policy, etc.) conducted at the national level. There is a European monetary union, which is not incorporated into a political union.

The crisis' crucial point, however, is not related to budgetary deficits, but to deep current account disequilibriums among the Eurozone countries, a consequence of huge increasing differences of competitiveness. As the euro's nominal exchange rate is fixed, a country cannot increase its international competitiveness by devaluing its currency. Thus, as there is a very strong correlation between 'unit labor costs,' the most important measure of international competitiveness, and inflation, with the implicit rule of a monetary union being that for each country, real wages can only increase following increases in its (each country's) productivity.

Between 2000 and 2010, Greece's net exports were sluggish, while domestic demand rose 2.3 percent (EU estimates), and real compensation to labor increased on average 1.9 percent per employee annually, a little less than productivity. Unit labor costs increased 30 percent between 2000 and 2010.

From the other side, since the euro's introduction, Germany has adopted a clear strategy of increasing its international competitiveness, accumulating a huge current account surplus. Between 2000 and 2007, Germany's current account results changed from an external deficit of 1.7 percent of the GDP to a surplus of 8 percent. What happened? Between 2000 and 2010, net exports exploded, while domestic demand increased only 0.2 percent yearly; real compensation growth stagnated at 0.4 percent yearly, far below productivity growth, causing employment creation to not follow due to wage restraint. Moreover, unit labor costs have grown only 5 percent in ten years.

In simple terms, the German cost of production of goods and services is practically the same as in 2000. This means that a comparable good or service produced at the same cost in 2000, in all Eurozone members and that could be sold at the same price, now costs 35 percent more to be produced in Greece, around 30 percent in Portugal, Spain, and Italy as well, 19 percent in France, and 23 percent in Ireland. In Latvia's case, from 2004 until 2010, this is around 80 percent, while in Estonia it is around 50 percent and in Lithuania 30 percent.

As Germany's government is making incredible pressure in wage negotiations to not increase unit labor costs in 2010, since devaluation is impossible in boosting competitiveness, the only solution is to cut real salaries. The consequence is well known: deflation and unemployment resulting in depression for the EU as a whole. Even if between 2010 and 2025 real wages increase 5 percent yearly in Germany, while only around 2 percent in other Eurozone countries, Germany will still have a privileged position, to the detriment of the other Eurozone countries. This may lead Portugal, Spain, Italy and Ireland to examine the option to abandon the euro.

It is impossible to economically survive when facing absolute disadvantages against the most important trade partner. The EU is Latvia's most important trade partner, while all economic policies are hostage of adopting the euro. It's time to think more pragmatically about the consequences of adopting the euro, taking in consideration the real economy, and not only the financial system.

Tax Reform and Economic Development: an Impossible Mission in Latvia?

Jun 17, 2010

In the last weeks, one question has been broadly discussed in Latvia: is a progressive tax regime good for Latvia? Several answers have been presented. Simplifying, while one group believes this is a good choice, as it shares prosperity and reduces social inequality, another believes a progressive tax system would result in people and firms paying more taxes. There are people saying it is against the free market and capitalism, even after the IMF has recommended a progressive tax system for the country. This is the joke of the year: the IMF is against the free market and capitalism.

An international comparison shows that the only countries that do not have a progressive tax regime are those of the former communist block, together with Iraq, Iceland, Mauritius, Jersey, and Guernsey, which are not the best examples of high levels of economic and social development. The most developed countries in the world, like the United States, Germany, Finland, Japan, all have progressive tax systems. These countries have understood that, although the free market is a precondition for achieving economic development, market forces cannot guarantee a distribution of income sufficient to all individuals and families to meet basic needs.

Nevertheless, even Milton Friedman, the main ideologue of the free-market as social demiurge, was convinced about the necessity of some kind of a progressive tax regime. In his 1961 book "Capitalism and Freedom," he developed the idea of a negative income tax system, an inverted progressive income tax, to guarantee a minimum income to poor families. Thus, although he supported the idea of a flat tax system, he believed families earning less than a determined minimum should receive payments from the government. Obviously, Milton Friedman knew perfect models exist only in theory and worried about the less favored. Something that does not occur in Latvia.

Latvia's tax system and most of its economic policies are ideologically determined by a specific, narrow, and sometimes equivocated understanding of neoliberalism, based on the conclusions of the Washington Consensus. First, it reflects a strategy of development based on what may be called "Flick Paradigm:"[1] In Latvia, it is very cheap to be rich, but very expensive to be poor. The idea is that not taxing the rich, at the same time not taxing financial

---

[1] Refers to airBaltic's former CEO Bertolt Flick.

activities, capital gains, real estate speculation, and other forms of unproductive economic activities, would attract investors, thus resulting in economic development. Second, the lack of compromise between politicians and some of Latvia's elite with the Latvian people. It is clear that part of these people's aversion to the idea of a progressive tax system is based on their own personal interests.

The question is that, in reality, a flat tax system is regressive. Although it seems that everybody is paying the same tax level, richer people are in reality paying relatively less than the poor. This occurs because of an often forgotten concept in economics called "marginal value of money." The idea is simple: the more money an individual has, the less is its relative value. In simple words, the value of 100 lats to someone who earns 300 lats a month is relatively much bigger than to someone who earns 2,000 lats.

Besides being socially unfair, a flat tax system does not guarantee economic development, either. Because of Latvia's economic model, it is not possible to use monetary policy to stimulate business. As a result, the only instrument we have to foster development is fiscal policy, which is much more than simply "the budget." It involves a complex system to achieve concrete goals of development, depending on different levels of taxation to stimulate investments. It is quite simple: tax the activities you do not want, free the ones you want. Also, recent studies have shown that since the 1990s, tax is increasingly becoming one of the most important factors for attracting foreign direct investment.

That is why Latvia should change its tax system. Not only regarding income, but also business activities and personal wealth. First, it is necessary to implement a progressive income tax system. This would have the same effect as increasing wages without increasing costs, helping Latvia to stop the work force from emigrating. Second, low rates and a simpler tax system on real business, privileging foreign direct investment and exporting companies. Third, a simplified system with real low tax levels to micro and small enterprises, instead of the joke presented by the government some months ago. Fourth, tax non-productive land and property. Fifth, increase the tax on capital gains and dividends. Sixth, tax wealth. In other words, tax oligarchs, speculators, and the financial system, instead of real business. Maybe this is something impossible to be done?

Latvia's Health Care System in Crisis

Aug 04, 2010

Much ink has been spilled about Latvia's health care system's problems. Nevertheless, the focus is usually on optimization and not on needed structural reforms. Naturally, optimization is very much needed. However, only a structural reform decentralizing the decisional process may result in a higher degree of resolvability, integration of actions, and quality. At the same time, it must proportionate a solution for its forthcoming worst financial problems, promote a more rational use of resources and, clearly define what is public and what is private, to avoid fraud and corruption.

First, there is the lack of a clear definition of what is public and what is private at the state level, a problem not only of the health system, but also of Latvia's state administrative structure. This is the result of the common misunderstanding in Latvia that the state apparatus can be administrated like a private company in all aspects. Although it is important to learn from the practices of the private sector, the fact that the money running the state apparatus is public money makes a huge difference.

In the case of Latvia's health system, since the early 1990's some health facilities have been privatized or partially privatized, while other institutions remain controlled by the state. This results in a wide variety of property ownership, making unclear what is public and what is private. The first step is to choose which institutions should remain under state control and which not. In the first case, it is also necessary to decide which institutions should be merged, aiming to optimize costs. After doing this, in strengthening this separation, it is also necessary to end the common practice of doctors using state-owned infrastructure for their private praxis. Instead, those institutions being fully privatized should be transformed into non-profit public institutions of private capital where doctors may have their private praxis.

A second aspect involves decentralization. Latvia experienced the decentralizing of its health system before, in the beginning of the 1990's. This experience is considered to be negative. Accordingly to the World Health Organization's publication "Latvia: Health System Review," the result was that there were different payment mechanisms for services, inefficient inter-district purchasing and allocation of equipment, just to cite a few. Another critical point was that local health managers tried to retain as much health care spending as possible to strengthen their own institutions. This resulted in a reluctance to refer patients to institutions outside the municipality. Therefore, the main problem was that the process of decentralization was not accompanied by necessary intervention in regulating it.

What should be done in these times of crisis is to decentralize the centralizing. Primary care must continue to be done through family doctors. However, the system must be decentralized, being the responsibility of municipalities as a way to reduce the bureaucratic charge of the central government. To change the focus from supply to demand, the support from the national level must be determined by the number of inhabitants of each municipality. This guarantees that demand determines the size of local supply. As each case is individual, it is necessary to establish a channel to deal with local demands, avoiding distortions that may result in prejudice to poorer regions. Secondary and tertiary care must be the responsibility of regional hospitals and polyclinics, which are to be the responsibility of the national government. The idea here is to concentrate these services in a few places, increasing economies of scale, and providing a more ample and better service for the population.

Another fundamental part of the reform is to increase the wages of personnel working directly with patients, including doctors. This is a fundamental step to end the culture of the envelope. Giving presents/money is often justified by the fact that doctors have small salaries. Although this may be true, it does not justify illegal payments that constitute private appropriation of state-owned installations. As the population begins to understand that doctors are well remunerated, it is to be expected that they will stop giving envelopes.

All these reforms cost money. In this case, there is a simple solution: impose a special health tax on financial transactions, of around 0.5 percent. This tax should not pass through the central budget, but directly to the Ministry of Health and should be audited by the State Control. Otherwise, the conditions of the health system will only worsen, because it is not to be expected that the budget for health will increase, but the contrary. Latvia still has to pay back the debt coordinated by the EU and IMF.

Cut to Grow?

Aug 19, 2010

Latvia's intelligentsia and policy makers are host of a very specific and simplistic understanding of politics and economics. Simplifying, thus incurring in the dangers of making simplifications, this can be divided into three complementary presuppositions. First, that economic liberalism is equal to political democracy, as George Stigler and Milton Friedman from the University of Chicago believed. Maybe this explains why they collaborated with General Pinochet's dictatorial regime. Second, that any kind of economic policy different from Latvia's own version of radical (neo)liberalism is tantamount to communism. Third, and as consequence of the first and the second, that the adoption of any policy different from those Latvia has been pursuing since its independence, even taking into consideration that it has resulted in this crisis, is equivalent to being against Latvia's independence, the Latvian language and the Open-Air Ethnographic Museum.

Following this logic, it's natural that, because of its intellectual myopia, the Latvian intelligentsia puts Keynes, Schumpeter, Sraffa, Robinson, among others, together with Lenin and Stalin, or, at best, with Latin America's populists of the 1950's. Thus, there is the establishment of a specific political conservative ideology based on a distorted notion of liberalism, which determines Latvia's pedestrian economic policies. This ideology is much reproduced and spread by the Latvian media.

A good example of the media's role in shaping ideological patterns is Pauls Raudseps' article 'Griez, lai Augtu' (Cut to Grow) published in IR last June. In this article, he defends two main ideas. First, that any form of economic stimulation is wrong because it's Keynesianism and results in budget deficits. Second, in the case of budget deficits, the financial market will not lend money to us, making it impossible for Latvia's economy to develop. The best is to not interfere in the economy. This is exactly the pedestrian economic approach that resulted in the current crisis. To support these ideas, he uses two papers from an economist from Harvard, Alberto Alesina. According to Raudseps' article, Alesina's papers prove empirically that fiscal consolidation automatically results in economic growth and that politicians who promote budget cuts are most probably to be re-elected. A more careful reading of Alesina's papers shows that things are not so simple.

First, Alesina's statistical methodology is problematic. For example, in the case of Japan, according to Adam S. Posen's "Restoring Japan's Economic Growth," the only significant stimulus plan ever made was in 1995. A look on

Alesina's appendix tables shows that 1995 is not there, while 2005 and 2007, when there weren't stimulus plans, are. Thus, Alesina "forgets" the clearest example of a large Keynesianism-based stimulus policy in recent history. Second, the full literature about economic stimulus assumes that the interest rates are up against the zero boundary; in other words, that it's a situation of liquidity trap. Alesina's analysis doesn't take this in consideration.

Rather, it treats 1990's Japan, which was up against the zero boundary, the same as countries that had high interest rates during the 1970's and the 1980's. It's different when the Central Bank adjusts interest rates in response to changing economic conditions and may raise rates to neutralize the effects of a fiscal expansion. Third, it implicitly presupposes that the government spending multiplier has always a small value. Some studies have shown that is not always the case.

The question of politicians being re-elected after budget cuts is true, but under specific conditions. The literature about political business cycles shows that there is a clear connection between macroeconomic performance and voting, although the economy is not the only factor explaining the latter. This means that while budget consolidation doesn't result in economic recession, incumbents are not penalized. The contrary is also true: if budget consolidation results in a recession, incumbents are penalized. As there is causality between Alesina's papers, it seems both are more ideological than serious research.

Are there any academic articles that answer these questions correctly? Yes. One is Christiano, Eichenbaum and Rebelo's "When is the Government Spending Multiplier Large?" Their research concludes that in a situation of biding a zero-interest-rate, government spending is very powerful in stimulating the economy. Another one is Almunia's "The effectiveness of fiscal and monetary stimulus in depressions," which uses data from the 1930's, a period of zero-rates, and defense spending. In both cases, the results are very Keynesian. To help Latvia in developing, the Latvian intelligentsia must go beyond its own reductionist ideology, and start to think more pragmatically. For example, understand that deficits are bad, but this doesn't mean that monetary and fiscal stimulus doesn't work as development instruments when done correctly.

I just would like to add, just in case, that I am for Latvia's independence, the Latvian language, and the Open-Air Ethnographic Museum.

All the W's of the World

Sep 22, 2010

In the last days, much has been discussed about the possibility that the world economy is passing through a W-shaped recession. This is the case when, after a first period of economic recession, there is a short period of growth followed by another period of recession. This was the case of the early 1980's recession in the United States, which officially began in July of 1981 and ended in November of 1982. It resulted from the combination of several factors, like the oil shocks of the 1970's, the process of contractionist monetary policies adopted by the U.S. Federal Reserve under Paul Volcker, and the process of deregulation known as "reaganomics."

Usually, economic activity is measured using the GDP as main indicator. However, this is not the most reliable one. Rather, it is better to rely upon other indicators, like industrial production and industrial capacity utilization, as they reflect the state of the real sector. Making a graphic analysis, it is possible to perceive several W's of various magnitudes and durations. Also, there are inter-W's, a situation of a W inside another W.[2]

In this case, it is possible to see there is a big W between 1973, the year of the first oil shock, and 1984, when the interest rates dropped to 11 percent after reaching a peak of 20.4 percent in 1981. In other words, this period's volatility reflects mostly the structural adjustments of the real sector, although the process of financial deregulation of the 1980's has its share in increasing the economic instability of that period. Nevertheless, if by that time the financial sector's influence was limited, now it is the determinant, as the world basic economic structure has changed.

The difference is that since the end of the Bretton Woods system and of the gold standard, which permitted the process of financial deregulation of the last 40 years, the financial system has split in two. As a result, instead of the simple and complete relationship between the real and financial sector, part of the latter is reproducing itself independently, without any direct contact with the real world. In other words, part of the financial system became detached from reality, assuming a casino-like configuration. To put it in concrete terms: in 2007, before the crisis, the world GDP (real sector) was USD 54.3 trillion; the part of the financial sector connected with the real world (bank assets, stock market capitalization and debt securities) was

---

[2] See http://www.federalreserve.gov/releases/g17/current/g17.pdf.

USD 178.4 trillion; but casino economics (derivatives) was 595.3 trillion, or more than ten times the world GDP.

Is this a problem? Yes. Why? Simple: because this money doesn't exist. It is a fiction supported by sophisticated econometric models and accounting tricks. As fiction, it is very unstable, as the reality perception and expectations of gamblers change very quick, as they realize the money they were supposed to have doesn't exist. This is called a correction. The problem is that the financial casino's corrections affect the part of the financial sector connected with the real world, reducing the necessary credit and financial intermediation supporting the real economy. The result is a real crisis.

The statistics of the U.S. Federal Reserve show that between the beginning of the crisis in 2007 and now, there are very clear W's in the production of durable goods, construction, energy and crude processing. This means that the real economy is supposed to be growing at a sustainable pace. This was confirmed by the recent announcement of the Business Cycle Dating Committee of the National Bureau of Economic Research (NBER), that July 2009 marks the end of the recession. This is good news for Latvia's few competitive exporting sectors. If we already had the expected W's, is it possible that a second wave of crisis will occur?

The answer is yes. However, it is not directly connected with the recent crisis. It is just that the system is very unstable. Thus, it's not the case to ask if there will be a second wave, but when a new crisis will happen. This last crisis was hugely influenced by the equity bubble of the late 1990's and the housing bubble of the beginning of the 2000's, in combination with people misestimating their wealth by referencing it to their equity portfolios, resulting in an artificially high level of consumption. The world economy is passing though a process of huge adjustment, resulting in instability. Some Wall Street economists believe it will last no less than 10 years.

Latvia's crisis has nothing to do with this. Although Parex made things worse, Latvia's crisis is a matter of (under)development. Let's not worry about the W's. We're too peripheral. Instead, let's start discussing development. For real.

'Schadenfreude' and Economic Development

Oct 21, 2010

China's manipulation of the renminbi is worrying the entire world about a currency war. This was aggravated by the increasing American anger over China's exchange policy. Accordingly to data published last Thursday by the US Census Bureau, the US trade deficit has climbed to - 46.3 billion dollars, from which 60.5 percent is with China. This is resulting in increasing pressures for labeling China as a currency manipulator by the US Treasury. In Germany, companies are complaining about what they consider China's aggressive strategy towards Europe. Germany's Industry's Committee on Easter Europe Economic Relations warned that China seems to be driven by geopolitical rather than economic interests. A number of other German businessmen strongly criticized China for its procurement practices, including forced transfers of technology and know-how in return for market access.

What China is doing is clear: it is following an aggressive development policy. Firstly, it is making its currency weak, as a way to boost exports. Secondly, China is forcing the transfer of technology and know-how, to really develop and become independent from Europe and the USA. Lastly, to counterbalance internal inflationary pressures, China is pursuing a contractionary domestic monetary policy to balance inflationary pressures, reducing global demand. As a result, China's development policies are hitting developed countries. The Germans call this 'Schadenfreude' (pleasure in others' pain).

What in reality is happening is still a mix of the hangover from the last financial crisis with the effects of the US economic recovery policies. Since the beginning of the crisis, the US and other developed countries have been increasing their monetary base, pursuing an aggressive monetary policy to spur growth. This pattern is expected to continue, even intensifying, as a result of the weak recovery observed, high unemployment and, in some cases, the possibility of deflation. Although neoclassical monetarism, the main ideology determining the economic policies of the last 40 years, presupposes that both monetary and fiscal policies should not be used to influence the economy, many countries have been using fiscal policy to stimulate their economy. However, because of financial limitations (large public debts combined with marker pressures) and political pressures (the resistance to increasing public expenditure), some advanced countries, including the US, are starting to pursue an aggressive monetary policy. Because of their increasing monetary base, their currencies are depreciating.

As developing countries, including the BRICs, have growth potential, large interest rate differentials, and open capital accounts, there is a massive shift of capital from developed to developing countries. As a result, these countries are facing rapid growth in credit, resulting in bubbles in the real estate market and consumption of durable goods, inflation, and demand. Moreover, their currencies are appreciating, making central banks adopt capital controls and other measures like increasing taxes on foreign capital. As these countries' exchange rates are free, their currencies are appreciating resulting in current account deficits. In other words, developed countries are exporting their way out of the crisis to developing countries. It is 'Schadenfreude' again.

Nevertheless, there is another aspect to be considered: the political. Many authors, such as Giovanni Arrighi, Andre Gunder Frank, and Immanuel Wallerstein, predicted that the world's current division of economic power would pend to the orient. This is already happening. The new thing is that for the first time there are explicit political reactions, as for example the pressures from the IMF and the European Commission asking China to revaluate its currency. This may result in a world broken into two economic blocs. One centered upon the US and the EU, and another upon the BRICs. Last month China supported Russia's idea of start direct trading using the renminbi and the ruble. It is negotiating similar deals with

Turkey and Brazil. This is not a currency war. It is a fight for development and economic dominance.

Crisis and State Reform in Latvia

Dec 08, 2010

At this moment, Latvia's most important political task is to establish a program of state reform. At the international level, between the 1930s and the 1960s, the state was a strong factor for promoting economic development. During this period, the level of economic and social welfare achieved levels never seen before. Nevertheless, in the beginning of the 1970s the state's exaggerated growth resulted in barriers to economic development. In other words, in inflation, stagnation, and unemployment. From the political side, the answer was the establishment of neo-conservatism as the chief ideology, expressed on the economic side as neo-liberalism and the promotion of the minimum state as paradigm. When Latvia became independent from the USSR in the beginning of the 1990s, it was just natural that the state was reformed with the basis of neo-conservatism and neo-liberalism.

However, if by the political side the Latvian state reflects neo-liberal ideology, its structural side still reproduces many forms of the Soviet state, which is a direct heritage of the Czarist state. As a result, Latvia's state apparatus, its bureaucratic structure, and its legal system are archaic and not able to face the real challenges the current crisis imposes on the country regarding sustainable economic development.

The first problem is political, and is a consequence of the process of rent seeking by many politicians and civil servants. The state is considered by them as a way of assuring their jobs or personal gains and advantages, as during the Soviet time. It is no surprise the maintenance of, and, in some cases the increase in, the "paperwork" culture, creating unnecessary administrative work - while making the army of civil servants appear necessary but at the same time making state services inaccessible to the average citizen – has led to protecting civil servants from working. Last, there is the convenience of transferring to the market the responsibility for what is the output of the actions and decisions of politicians and civil servants.

The second is the debility of the model of state intervention, reflecting the inefficacy of neo-liberalism to promote development. If forty years before the problem was within the Keynesian state and the multiplication of subsidies and excess of regulations, nowadays the problem is the messianic faith in the financial market as substitute for the real sector and the state in the coordination of economic development. The third problem is the inefficiency of the state administrative apparatus reflecting a state that has grown, but has not become strong; rather, on the contrary, has become big and weak, thus not able to fulfill its basic functions, including to complement and correct market failures as, yes, the market sometimes fails, and Latvia is a good example.

The fourth problem is also the worst: it is the fiscal crisis of the state. It should not be confounded with populist budgetary irresponsibility or with the occasional fiscal deficit that results from some mistake. Rather, the fiscal crisis is a structural problem reflecting both the real economy's lack of development and the capture of the state. Although persistent public deficits can result in fiscal crisis, the problem is when public savings start to be used to pay the external and internal public debts' interest, instead of being used to promote economic development. This is exactly Latvia's case, which will have to use public savings, including privatizing public companies, to pay the external debt instead of modernizing the health and educational system, for example. In Latvia's case, this is aggravated by its regressive tax system and the lack of proper supervision by the competent authorities.

State reform is a precondition to solve the fiscal crisis and to solve the model of intervention's debility and the inefficiency of the apparatus of the State. However, it is a political decision. Without political support it will never happen. The fundamental point is that Latvia needs a modern, professional and efficient state observing the needs of the citizens and business, a managerial state, where patrimonialism and bureaucratism are condemned. The objective of the state reform should not be to achieve the minimum state. Rather, to reduce it while defining new strategies of development, in a manner to boost the state capacity to help develop business. If even Brazil was able to do it under certain limits, Latvia can do the same. It is just a matter of being more pragmatic and less religious regarding Latvia's politicians and some economists' predominant economic beliefs.

Neo-liberal Populism and the State. Who is Really Rational?

Jan 13, 2011

Since the 1970s, we have learned that the state was the source of everything bad happening in the economy. We learned that the private sector was always in equilibrium because of the market forces, while the state was always subjected to economic populism. This idea has its origins in Adam Smith's concept of the invisible hand, later complemented by Bentham's utilitarianism. The idea is quite simple: each individual is looking rationally for his/her own personal well-being; as a result, the conjunction of each individual action results in an optimal social and economic situation in which any external interference, principally from the government, disturbs this perfect state of things. Other important presuppositions are that each individual has free access to all information upon which to base their decisions, that services and products can be perfectly substituted for another, and that there are no monopolies or oligopolies.

In concrete terms, the corollary of this unreal theoretical

framework is a set of economic policies turned into dogmas by politicians with the help of the media and some people of the academic sector. Among these beliefs, one is that budget deficits are always the result of populist politicians, who expend money only to please their electorate and get re-elected. Besides this presupposition being anti-democratic, the financial crisis of the last 30 years has shown that the market never was able to control the private agent's speculative behavior.

It is not the case to say that there are no populist politicians. Nevertheless, if in majority, they are responsible. Take a look in the statistics of national deficits. In most cases, the governments were following responsible policies; the irrational behavior was in the private sector, with its real estate bubbles and speculation with derivatives. What must be clear is that the recent budget deficits some countries are experiencing are the result of the private sector's irrationality and not because of populism. In the case of a financial crisis, the state helps the banks, thereby increasing the public deficit in order to avoid the economy collapsing. Then, it increases its expenses to maintain the aggregate demand to support the level of public confidence.

Ireland is a very good example. The government had the deficit under control. Even the public debt was reduced from 30 percent to 25 percent of GDP before the crisis. Nevertheless, with the crisis and with the government having to support the Irish financial system, the public deficit increased to 65 percent of GDP in 2009, while preliminary data shows that it is expected to be 99 percent of GDP in 2010.

The conclusion is fair: the government is more rational than the private sector. But then there is one question: what private sector are we talking about? For sure, not about the productive sector. Rather, this sort of irrationality is characteristic of the financial sector. It is fuelled by the blind faith of politicians on the ability of the market to distribute economic resources in an optimal way. In other words, in the idea that if the government interferes in the economy, the result will be underinvestment due to economic populism.

The economic model adopted by the European Union heavily relies on the idea that the financial system should coordinate the distribution of economic resources in the private sector. In combination with responsible fiscal policies by the government, this would guarantee economic development, it is believed. Therefore, in Jose Manuel Barroso's own words, "without fiscal consolidation we will not have growth for a very simple reason: There will be no confidence. Without confidence, no investment; without investment, no growth." (International Herald Tribune, Dec. 29, 2010). But this is exactly the same model that resulted in the crisis. The financial sector did not distribute economic resources effectively, forcing governments, which were running fiscally responsible policies, to step in and bail out the banks, putting private sector debts in the lap of the public sector, helping to worsen the crisis. Fiscal consolidation has therefore been made that much harder by the profligacy of the private sector.

Latvia is host of the same logic. During the People's Party government, although the economy was growing, it wasn't developing. Rather, it was experiencing the deepening of structural imbalances. The authorities, including the Bank of Latvia and the Financial and Capital Market Commission, didn't deal with the crisis properly, as it would have been against neo-liberal ideology, thus against the Latvian language and the Open Air Ethnographic Museum. However, the problem is more profound. As the economy was growing, the parties of the coalition experienced very high degrees of approval. Instead of pursuing policies to deal with the unsustainable process Latvia's economy was passing through because of the private sector's irrationality, they surfed on the wave and received 59 seats in the 9th Saeima. Latvia's politicians are so incredible that they were even able to create a new form of populism: the neo-liberal one.

Defending Nationalism

Feb 10, 2011

The United States' foreign policy is based on the idea of what is called 'American Exceptionalism.' In reflection, this is the idea that this country is qualitatively different from other nations, as observed by Alexis de Tocqueville. Based on this presupposition, a specific ideology was established, based on the ideas of liberty, egalitarianism, individualism, populism (here in the sense of the U.S. populist movement in which farmers and other workers established their anti-trust agenda a little more than 100 years ago), and laissez-faire. This idea is closely tied to the 'Manifest Destiny,' which manifests the belief in the United States' mission to promote and defend democracy around the world. It is based on three main points: a) the virtue of the people from the United States and its institutions; b) the mission to spread these institutions, thus making the world the image of the United States; and c) the destiny under God to accomplish this work. These principles have much influenced U.S. foreign policy, including in the Middle East.

The main problem is that this evangelical impulse to spread freedom, democracy, and economic liberalism has been used sometimes as an instrument to defend nationalist interests. Several U.S. administrations have been supporting Mubarak's regime, and at the same time unsuccessfully pushing for reforms in Egypt. This includes the Obama administration. Notwithstanding Obama's Cairo speech, when he said that "(...) the ability to speak your mind and have a say in how you are governed; confidence in the rule of law and the equal administration of justice; government that is transparent and doesn't steal from the people the freedom to live as you choose. Those are not just American ideas, they are human rights, and that is why we will support them everywhere," Mubarak has been ignoring Obama's call for an orderly transition in government.

Mubarak's strategy is obvious. He is standing on the perception that any abrupt change may destabilize the entire region, allowing room for a theocratic regime a la Iran in 1979. As a result, there would not be many alternatives, as Mubarak's regime (and Saudi Arabia) has been a proxy for U.S. influence in the region, an influence hard to sustain, though.

Nevertheless, there is an alternative: the United States can be a friend with Turkey and Iran, and at the same time loosen its ties with Saudi Arabia, Israel, and Egypt. As Stephen Kinzer puts it in his book "Reset: Iran, Turkey and

America's Future," Turkey and Iran are the only countries in the Middle East where democracy is deeply rooted, making both countries logical partners' of the U.S.

Nevertheless, for such a change to be possible, it is necessary for qualitative changes to occur at the ideological level, making development a real objective of U.S. foreign policy. During the Neoliberal years (1979-2010), developed countries often condemned the underdeveloped countries' economic nationalism as something as bad and wrong, as ethnic nationalism, while they (the developed countries) pursued nationalist economic policies themselves. It is the usual strategy: you must do what I say and not what I do. The result is that the development gap nowadays is deeper than it was 40 years ago (see the U.N. World Economic and Social Survey 2010).

Although economic nationalism and liberalism may seem to be opposite ideas, they are complementary ideologies. It was by their combination that France, the United States, and Great Britain assured their process of development. In these countries, still today, the vast majority of inhabitants have no doubt that the State must defend the national interests. When underdeveloped countries use religion to strengthen their nationalism, they are using it to promote national unity, helping to achieve economic and social development.

Latvia, by her time, employs several nationalist strategies to promote national cohesion. Nevertheless, economic nationalism is considered to be against Latvia's interests. Politicians and many of my colleagues from the universities still believe that development is something occurring automatically, following the naive idea that, if we are good to others, others will be good to us. They think investors will invest here just because we did our homework and we're good, even if there are several countries within the European Union offering a much better investment environment. And, by investment here, it should be understood as productive investment and not just financial operations. Latvia's people's answer has been simple: instead of making revolutions like in Egypt, people are migrating to countries where, like Obama said, there is confidence in the rule of law, the government is transparent, and there are opportunities for them.

There are two messages here. One for the developed countries and one for Latvia. For the developed countries it is: let the underdeveloped countries develop. They will modernize, establish new institutions, observe human rights, among other things, making the world much more stable. For Latvia, it is time to be a little more pragmatic. It is time to, besides the Open Air Ethnographic Museum and the Latvian language, use every possibility to defend the national economic interests, to make government transparent, to increase the confidence in the rule of law. Only in this way can we survive as nation.

We Still Can Develop. Please Hurry Up!

Mar 09, 2011

Several authors have discussed economic development in the 20th century. The most relevant are Ragnar Nurkse, Paul Rosenstein-Rodan, Albert Hirschmann, Sir Arthur Lewis, Walt Rostow, Raul Prebisch, and Celso Furtado. Instead of constructing models disconnected from reality and based on philosophical presuppositions that cannot be demonstrated empirically, these economists were pragmatic men interested in concrete results. Most of them worked in the United Nations' system or in multilateral agencies with the concrete objective of promoting economic development.

Basically, these authors shared the belief that a) development policies should take into consideration the individual characteristics of each country; b) development tricks are not difficult; c) the time to develop is relatively short; d) the market is a means to achieve development and is not an end in itself. In concrete terms, they believed that, in the case of an underdeveloped country like Latvia, the profit-loss calculations of private entrepreneurs is too limited to induce development at the national level, like our recent history of approximately 1/3 of the Latvian economy being speculation with real estate and consumption of durable goods (cars, refrigerators, computers, etc.) has demonstrated.

Thus, the only way to achieve development would be to promote a 'big push' of concurrent investments in key sectors launching a chain reaction resulting from synergistic interaction. Only a massive injection of new technologies, new machines, new equipment, and new production processes across a vast range of economic sectors can result in development. One important point, as resources are limited, is that some sectors must be prioritized. However, because of chain linkages, investments in one sector spread to another, pushing the entire economy up.

Although popular during the 1950s and 1960s, because of the ideological cycle in economics, these ideas have been forgotten. Of course, there was also the problem of some countries incurring budget deficits and printing or borrowing money to finance development irresponsibly. Even taking into consideration that these policies resulted in crisis, the structural development jump these countries experienced is undeniable.

However, Latvia does not need to be irresponsible, pursuing populist economic policies.

Latvia has an advantage other developing countries do not have: it is a member of the European Union and still has some assets to privatize. First, the distribution of EU funds must reflect a concrete policy of development. Although Latvia has a document called the "Development Plan," it is more like a mission statement. It does not answer the question "how." Second, some sectors, such as telecommunications and electricity, must be privatized, following the model of 'concessions.' Although most probably the IMF will make very strong pressure for the money received to be used to pay the debt, and may even use blackmail, saying that "investors will lose confidence," the government must resist and use this money to promote development.

Although it sounds relatively simple, it is not. There are three structural barriers. The first one is the lack of human resources. Latvia simply does not have people sufficiently trained to deal with development policies at the state level. Latvia's authorities and civil servants have no clue on mechanisms of development. It isn't that they are not competent. It's just they do not have adequate training and knowledge.

The second one is the lack of policy coordination among different institutions. It is necessary to centralize the administration of economic resources and development planning in one institution only. First, as the Mortgage and Land Bank is turning into an investment bank, it should be responsible for administrating all financial resources related to development, including the EU's structural funds.

Second, the LIAA (development agency) should increase its focus on promoting entrepreneurship internally, and at the micro and small levels, while the Ministry of Foreign Affairs should be responsible for attracting foreign direct investment and promoting Latvian products abroad. As a result, LIAA offices in foreign countries can be closed, saving money.

The third one is related to the external environment. From one side, there are pressures from countries, which are not really interested in our development. It is not the case of believing in conspiracy theories or that these countries want us to be underdeveloped. Rather, it is just business as usual. They just do not care about our development. They will fight to defend their national interests. It is our choice to defend ours. From the other, Latvia is very worried about security, which is completely understandable. But the point is that, at this moment, the biggest threat for the Latvian language, culture, and the Open-Air Ethnographic museum is the lack of development. Please, hurry up!

Outsourcing is the Solution

May 18, 2011

Economic policies have an ideological, cyclical pattern following a crisis. From the beginning of capitalism, at the end of the 18th century until the 1930s, it was Classic Liberalism; from the 1930s until the 1970s it was Keynesianism; from the 1970s until now it has been Neoliberalism ideology. The main difference among these models is how the state regulates the economy. During Classic Liberalism, the state really did not interfere much in the economy. It was paradise for snake-oil salesmen and other rascals.

An interesting case during this period is the one of the Erie Railroad, running from the New Jersey side of the Hudson River to Buffalo. Cornelius Vanderbilt, transport tycoon and founder of Vanderbilt University in the U.S., controlled the New York Central on the east margin of the river. He wanted to own Erie Railway to guarantee a monopoly of railway service to Buffalo, and possibly Chicago. As some economic historians remark, his commitment was to robbing the public. The lasting contribution of his family to spoken language was the expression "The public be damned."

Vanderbilt's rivals were Jim Fisk, Daniel Drew, and Jay Gould. They were committed to robbing the stockholders by directing Erie Railway's cash and other assets to their own pockets. Controlling a company was the key for assuring a monopoly or to fill one's pocket. In 1867, what is known as the Erie War, started.

Vanderbilt hoped to acquire control of Erie by buying stock. Nevertheless, Drew and Fisk not only had control of the company, but also a printing press. As a result, they could print more stock than Vanderbilt was able to buy. Vanderbilt turned to the courts, where he had an advantage: he was in personal possession of George Gardner Barnard of the New York State Supreme Court, someone described as the "best that money can buy," who threatened Fisk, Drew and Gould with jail. They picked up the company's books and cash and flew across the river to Jersey City. Vanderbilt then started making efforts to kidnap them to bring them back to Judge Barnard's jurisdiction. A defense force was recruited from the railway yards, a flag was hung up and Taylor's Hotel, where they were established, was renamed "Fort Taylor."

They counterattacked, buying enough of the New York State Legislature to make the stock they printed legal. Later, they bought Judge Barnard himself, not only with money but naming a locomotive after him. The final beat was buying William Tweed, the head of Tammany Hall, the city affiliate of the Democratic Party controlling most of New York's elections. Vanderbilt retreated and peace was made.

Neoliberalism is not liberalism. It attempts to artificially emulate the conditions of perfect competition. In other words, Neoliberalism presupposes a strong state regulating the market to avoid Vanderbilts taking advantage of honest people. In other words, a strong state is needed to assure equal opportunity and a fair and transparent economic and political environment.

Latvia's understanding of Neoliberalism is tantamount to an extremely weak state. The result is an economic and political environment similar to 19th century New York. As a result, one can change the surnames Vanderbilt, Fisk, Drew or Gould to the ones of some Latvian politicians. For example, there's the case of Vitol Group prosecuting Ventspils Mayor Aivars Lembergs in the United Kingdom. This is the same as to say that Latvia's judicial system is not trustful.

When we start to discuss changing the tax system, the winning argument is always that any change will increase tax evasion. If the case is about increasing taxes on vodka and cigarettes, contraband will explode. We can't make real state reform, not only because of political feudalism, but because civil servants themselves are against it. We don't have real monetary policy and fiscal policy because the authorities are always finding excuses: "it's the impossible trinity," "we can't upset the banks," "we're a market economy."

The fact is that Latvia's state is unable to guarantee the basic needs of a neoliberal economy. In other words, Latvia's state is weak. It cannot control its borders, the law applies only for chicken thieves, the state health system has been captured by the "white mafia" who use state assets for personal gains, education at all levels has doubtful quality, there are doubts about the transparency of the judicial system.

Latvia outsourced its defense to NATO. Now, there are discussions about outsourcing part of customs control to Estonia. The fact is that Latvia's politicians and civil servants are unable to run the country. They aren't competent enough. That's why the only solution is to outsource Latvia's public administration, judicial system, and legislature to a third country like Sweden or Germany. Maybe to the EU. The faster we admit this, the best for the country, and the Latvian culture and language.

The Magic is Lost

Jul 06, 2011

Since when I was making my bachelor studies in Economics, I have developed a great interest in Political Economy. For readers from Eastern Europe, Political Economy usually is connected with Leninism-Stalinism, the distorted aberration of Marx's ideas that gave base to the Soviet Union. However, Political Economy is more than this. It is the study of economic ideas and its relationship with social reality, including the influence of politics in economic life.

Thus, it is not restricted to leftist ideas. Rather, socialist and communist ideas are part of the Political Economy's debate, as free market and liberalism also are. Radical right-wing economists like Ludwig von Mises, Friedrich von Hayek, and Milton Friedman also considered they were doing Political Economy. For example, one of the most prestigious academic journals in economics is Chicago University's "Journal of Political Economy," where Milton Friedman published several articles, such as his "A Theoretical Framework for Monetary Analysis," in 1970.

To put it simply, Political Economy is not about Marx or socialism. It's the study of economic ideas: their origins, their philosophical base, and, extremely important, their logic. Unfortunately, real logic is something very rarely taken into consideration in the economic debate nowadays. Of course, there is some logic when discussing economics, but it is too superficial. One example is both the European Union and Latvia's plan for development. The logic is that fiscal consolidation results in boosting financial markets' confidence, thus investment. As a result, the magic of development is guaranteed.

This was very well explained by Jose Manuel Barroso: "without fiscal consolidation we will not have growth for a very simple reason: There will be no confidence. Without confidence, no investment; without investment, no growth." (International Herald Tribune, December 29, 2010).

The idea is as follows: a consolidated budget guarantees financial stability; with financial stability, there are investments; with investments, there is growth and voila: Barroso is right. This is the same logic Prime Minister Valdis Dombrovskis' ghostwriter, Anders Aslund, used in their book. This is a very seductive axiom. I can see people shaking their heads positively when hearing it and even thinking "This guy is brilliant. I read the same thing in the newspaper."

However, the assumption that a consolidated budget

automatically results in development is false. There's no empirical evidence in the economic literature of such direct causality, even in writings of the most apologetic believers in neoclassical economics. Thus, it's an opinion and not economic science. What the academic economic literature shows is that there's a causality between consolidated budgets and the easiness of the state financing public debt by issuing bonds. The idea is simple. If the budget has a surplus, the government will be able to repay the bonds' nominal value, thus it's a secure investment. In other words, the government can finance public debt in the private financial system.

Why would it result in development? Because, if competently used, public debt is one of the most important instruments of development. It results in investments in infrastructure and social policies. Unfortunately, this is not Latvia's case, as our surplus will have to be used to pay for our debts. Although claiming in his latest book to be the Harry Potter of economics, what has Valdis Dombrovskis' government accomplished until now? First, public debt exploded from 23.91 percent to 43.01 percent of GDP. Second, internal devaluation is not working. Production costs have been increasing in the last six months. In comparison with their low in November 2009, they were already 15 percent higher in May 2011. Nominal wages are again at the same level as in July 2008, while real wages are at the same level as in September 2008.

Overall, Latvia's price index reached its low point in December 2009, but now it is already higher than in the beginning of 2009. In other words, Latvia's internal devaluation happened between March and December 2009, when prices started growing again. Finally, taking into consideration oil prices, deflation would have to be more intense than it was.

Am I missing something? Where is Valdis Potterovskis' magic? First, Latvia's crisis was basically of liquidity and not of solvency, which was solved by the IMF. That's why the financial market remained so calm. In the next years we'll see if we'll have a crises of solvency similar to Greece or not. So, 'nasing speshial.'

Second, it's lost in the lack of real structural reforms, including the much needed administrative reform of the state to reduce the costs of doing business in Latvia. I'm convinced Dombrovskis himself very much wanted to do these reforms. The problem has been always the coalition with Lembergs, sorry, with the Green and Rustics Union (ZZS), the guys who made Zatlers ask for the dissolution of the parliament. In macroeconomics, if you cannot help, then please don't disturb.

Development: Learning from previous Mistakes?

Aug 03, 2011

There is a saying that one must learn from his or her mistakes. Some months ago, President Barack Obama announced that the USA will create a development bank similar to the Brazilian National Bank of Social and Economic Development, to finance energy, sanitation, and transport infrastructure projects. This is strange. After all, the USA has been championing Neoliberal policies for several years, supporting general deregulation, liberalization, privatization, all in the name of the allegedly uber-rationality of the market, one based on surreal mathematical models. Is the USA turning its back to Neoliberalism and starting to look to the infamous developmentalism, after 40 years?

In reality, the case is that the USA is finally recognizing what the economic academia, even the most ideologically blind guys in Chicago, have known for years: that markets are imperfect, thus perfect competition doesn't exist. The fact is that the concept is just useful as a teaching instrument to explain basic economics, and should never be used as a basic presupposition to real-world economic policies. Neoliberalism is not only based on the idea that perfect competition is the norm, but also on the notion that the financial sector is both rational and stable, from the economic development perspective.

The current world economic crisis is a direct consequence of this belief. Putting it clearly, it would be sufficient to provide a stable macroeconomic environment, from the financial market point of view. This is what the USA, the European Union (but not Germany), and Latvia have been doing. Empirical evidence shows that the price paid for this choice is economic stagnation. While China invests 8 percent of its GDP in infrastructure, the USA invests only 2 percent. The result is clear: in the last 30 years the USA's GDP grew 1.7 times, while China's 17.7. Of course, the USA is expected to have a lower GDP growth rate, as it's in another stage of development. But such a huge difference can be explained only as the output of mistaken economic policies that saw the market opposed to the state, as in the USA's case. Although Wall Street seems to be vigorous even in times of crisis, the USA's real economy is not doing well.

The fact is that a weak state doesn't generate a strong market. It's the cooperation between both that results in development. Any development plan in Latvia should take this into consideration.

First, the government must be the agent responsible for defining a strategy of national development; it is the key institution for development. It's the state's duty to create investment opportunities. Second, reforms must be directed to strengthen the state and the markets. In his case, the administrative reform of the state is fundamental to changing the role of the state. Third, the state must have a limited and strategic industrial policy, mostly focusing on creating new business, increasing productivity, and technological modernization.

At the same time, it also must try to neutralize the tendency of wages growing more than productivity and the overvaluation of the real exchange rate. Fourth, development must be financed by foreign direct investment in the real sector, and/or internal savings. Fifth, macroeconomic policy should focus on three points concomitantly: inflation, the real exchange rate, and employment. The three are fundamental for development. Sixth, the fiscal standard must be defined very rigorously regarding public deficits and public savings.

Again, before reforming its fiscal policy, Latvia must face the administrative reform of the state. Seventh, the exchange rate must be floating, but managed inside the +- 15 percent corridor permitted by the Maastricht criteria, aiming for the industrial equilibrium exchange rate, the one making sophisticated manufacturing industries viable, thus avoiding the effects of the Dutch disease. Eighth, the government, the Bank of Latvia, and the Financial and Capital Market Commission, in case of necessity, shall actively limit the influence of the financial markets in the national economy to avoid over-heating and speculation. Ninth, both budget and current account deficits should be rejected, mainly on the trade and services accounts. Tenth, a fiscal reform is needed, reducing taxes on the poor. This is important, as it increases their income without incurring in increasing industrial costs. This boosts the consumption of local products.

The idea is simple. Standard barbershop economics restricts the concept of stability to the interests of the financial market, thus only restricting public expenses and inflation. The key is to include asset price stability, the equilibrium of the balance of payments, and the notion of full employment. We need to reject the idea that a primary surplus without structural reforms is enough. It only results in foreign over-indebtedness and financial fragility.

Finally, discussions started in Latvia, also within several parties, about a more active role of the state in promoting development. Let's hope the shortsighted radicals won't convince policy-makers that these policies are tantamount to Marxism-Leninism, or against the Ethnographic Open-Air Museum.

Privatize What to Develop Who?

Aug 31, 2011

Last week there was a very interesting discussion at Hotel Latvija. There were three guests: Ģirts Rungainis from Latvia, Morten Lallevig and Erik Reinert from Norway. The main question was about privatization and economic development. Personally, I have great interest in this theme, as I have researched and written extensively about the Brazilian privatization program, specifically about the role of foreign capital and its influence on the process of economic denationalization. The conclusion is not a surprise: low technology and low value-added sectors weren't of special interest to foreign investors. They were really interested in the sectors with high technological levels, such as telecommunications and aviation, the natural monopolies, like electricity distribution, and, of course, the state banks.

The arguments supporting the idea of privatization were the same as presented in Latvia and can be divided in three groups. First, the technological one. With the tremendous technological innovation of the last 40 years, the state is not necessary anymore for promoting competition among firms. Rather, the technology generated by the private sector creates the necessity to change the role of the state, from producing goods and services, to regulating markets. Another factor connected with technological development is the flexibilization of the productive process, where productive units are increasingly smaller and globally coordinated. As a result, many of the nationalized commanding heights, which were conceived under the mass production model, cannot compete with countries like China, therefore being necessary to privatize them.

The second group of arguments is the economic one. Its core rationale is related to increasing competition and the maximization of efficiency in producing and distribution of public goods and services. The idea is that market forces are more efficient than the state in generating production of specific goods and services. In other words, the private sector would be more efficient because it is subject to competition and because it is free from state bureaucracy. Another point is connected with the idea of macroeconomic stability, as state-owned companies have been considered to be deficitary, thus increasing the fiscal dis-equilibrium. If not creating dis-equilibrium, these companies would at least absorb resources from the central budget that could be allocated to social programs. Thus, privatization would be necessary to reduce the budget deficit and the public debt. It would also solve the problem of performance, as these firms would follow market forces.

The third group of arguments is the political-ideological. The idea is simple: privatization democratizes the economy, as it promotes a more ample and just division of property, thus permitting the participation of a bigger share of the population in controlling strategic industrial sectors such as, for example, shareholders. Thus, sectors like telecommunications.

With such powerful arguments for privatizing, there is something difficult to understand: why in Latin America were most of the telecommunication and energy companies bought by state-owned companies from other countries, like Electricite de France and Telefonica de Espana? First, because the commanding heights have changed from basic industrial sectors to those connected to the knowledge society, like telecommunications. Second, because some of these companies are natural monopolies, like electricity and natural gas, resulting in high profits because, well, they are monopolies. Third, because empirical evidence has shown that these arguments are flawed.

The first, because in the most developed countries technological development still is financed mainly by the state for one simple motive: research and development is extremely expensive. That's why most of the research occurs in universities, funded if not totally, then partially by public resources. The second, because not all state-owned companies are inefficient and/or run deficits, thus, their profits can be used for social policies. The third, because history has shown that small shareholders sold their shares quickly, so there is no democracy, just usual business. Also, because, for example, tariffs of public services went up strongly after privatization, reducing both industrial competitiveness and household purchasing power, while pushing inflation up.

Telia, a Swedish state-owned company, has been pressuring Latvia to privatize their state-owned telecommunications companies. These companies are in good shape. They are efficient and very profitable. Latvia has no real motivation for privatizing them. It's a matter of economic colonization. LMT and Lattelecom can be part of a pragmatist industrial policy to establish a technological cluster, boosting development and economic growth. Swedish people are very clever. They want to buy our companies, so we can make them richer. I have another idea. Let's start defending our interests. Let's develop. And then, let's start pressuring Sweden to sell Telia to Lattelecom or LMT, using the same arguments they use, so the Swedes can make us rich. Instead of being an economic colony, let's colonize others.

You Made Your Bed, Now Lie in It

Nov 10, 2011

Last August Latvia's Central Statistics Bureau published statistics on emigration. It reached a record: 2,300 individuals, or 0.12 percent, of Latvia's population left the country looking for a better life in August alone. Leaving the human aspect aside, in economic terms this is a disaster: in practice, Latvia's workforce is moving away, reducing the possibilities for development because of lacking workforce. This is one of the main indicators of economic failure: emigration. Of course, the world is very curious to understand how the Latvian government was able to implement an austerity economic plan without the riots seen in Greece. This has been because people are just leaving the country.

Our Prime Minister Valdis Dombrovskis has a plan called the "Dombrovskis Plan." I must agree that, in face of the other parties' plans, it is an advance in the debate on development. For example, the Zatlers Reform Party's economic plan is to basically, well, you can guess: we are not liberal enough, thus we need a wave of further liberalization, end all subsides and have no industrial policy.

Nevertheless, the prime minister's plan has serious problems and is contradictory in some points. I've sent a long letter addressing these issues to the guys responsible for the plan, including Valdis Dombrovskis himself. The only answer I got was a formal "thank you for sending your comments" from someone I don't know. Thus, I'm making my comments public, so everybody can know what these problems are and maybe to foster some debate about economic policy.

First, there's no differentiation between the concepts of growth and development. As economics is an ideological discipline, some schools of thought, including the most important nowadays - Chicago Neoclassic Monetarism - consider both concepts as synonyms. They aren't. Economic growth doesn't necessarily result in development. Remember Latvia between 2004 and 2008? It's clear there wasn't any development. Development results from structural changes and can be easily measured by what a country exports. Sweden exports Volvo cars and trucks, Ericsson telecommunication equipment, just to cite a few. With very few exceptions, we export wood.

Second, the plan is inflationary, as it foresees investments of around 1 billion lats in development in the next years, which will increase Latvia's monetary base. Just to recall, Latvia's inflation increased from 6.57 percent in 2006 to 15.25 percent in 2008, as a direct consequence of the monetary base (M2) increasing from 5.46 billion lats to

6.40 billion lats. I don't have to remind anyone that adopting the euro is considered Latvia's economic Graal and the solution for all our problems. But, if we start developing and investing, we'll have inflation. With inflation there will be no euro. There'll be the euro for underdeveloped countries such as Latvia, though they are already talking about expelling Greece from the club and making the Eurozone to be only for VIP countries.

Third, this plan's central strategy is to adopt the euro. The idea is simplistic: the euro will give us macroeconomic stability, thus we'll have investments and economic growth, thus development. The idea presupposes that financial institutions will feel more confident in investing their money in Latvia, boosting credit. This rationale is flawed. Let's just remember what happened between 2004 and 2008. It's a direct consequence of the fact that what is good for the financial system isn't always good for the real economy. That's why the academic economic literature shows that the determinants of productive investment differ from those of financial investment. In other words, the determinants of productive investment are different from those determining financial investment.

For example, availability of workforce is one of the most important factors determining investment. That's why emigration is extremely problematic. Other factors are access to markets, cost structure (including taxes on the workforce), construction costs, and subsides. However, transport and telecommunications are not very important. Also, and specifically for Latvia because of its small internal market, a weak exchange rate is very effective for boosting exports. Thus, although for the financial sector a stable exchange rate is very important, to the real sector it can be a problem if the real exchange rate is becoming too strong; by the way, this is exactly Latvia's case.

Focusing on pleasing the financial markets and adopting the euro aren't solutions. The same goes with advertising our products abroad. It doesn't change our productive structure or our level of productivity.

The economic crisis the world is passing through is exactly about this. The countries that favored the financial sector, like Latvia, Iceland, Ireland, and even the USA, are facing crisis. The countries that favored the real economy and the productive sector, like Germany, China, Brazil, and India, are doing well. In economics, it's quite clear: you made your bed, now lie in it. Or, as President Bill Clinton once said, "It's the economy, stupid." I hope politicians will understand while there is still time.

Pinocchio and the Economic Crisis

Dec 07, 2011

Much has been written by pundits and organizations about the causes and consequences of the current Eurozone crisis. Some defended the idea that poor banking regulation results in speculation and bubbles; others that Germany is guilty of increasing its productivity while keeping real wages almost constant during the last 10 years, thus boosting its exports while financially hurting other Eurozone members because of the balance of payments; a third one, and maybe the most popular, is that public debt was financed by banks until reaching an unsustainable level. All of them are true. The problem is that they only deal with the appearance of a deeper problem: economic populism.

"It's the economy, stupid" is a phrase widely used during Bill Clinton's 1992 campaign. Although the original idea was to refer to Clinton as a better choice than George Bush, senior, to address the economic recession the USA was facing, it turned to symbolize the free market and the notion that politicians aren't directly responsible for what happens in the economic arena. This is a very attractive idea for politicians. A convenient lie. If "it's the economy, stupid," they aren't responsible at all. Nonsense.

Although it's true that there is a relatively free market, in reality there are norms and regulations so as to avoid moral hazard. As a result, the economic agents will maximize their gains accordingly to specific norms, rules, and legislation. But who makes the rules and norms? The politicians, the same people trying to convince us they aren't responsible, but the economy. Jose Manuel Barroso is one of the champions of this kind of nonsense. According to him, Portugal's crisis was the result of Moody's downgrading the Eurozone's credit rating. He then suggested the creation of a rating agency controlled by Brussels' bureaucracy...

Unfortunately, after reading the news, it is possible to realize that politicians are lying most of the time, including about the Eurozone. In a recent interview with The Daily Telegraph, Jacques Delors, the former president of the European Commission, stated that the euro was doomed since the beginning. Accordingly to him, politicians have chosen to not take into consideration the fundamental structural problems and imbalances of member states. More, that Eurozone finance ministers "did not want to see anything disagreeable for which they would be forced to deal with."

The fact is that this crisis is the result of old-fashioned irresponsible populism. Since the 1980s, there's been strong support for measures limiting economic populism. One of the most important is the independence of central banks. The idea is simple: politicians will run deficits to achieve electoral goals. To finance these deficits, they would force their countries' central banks to print money, increasing the monetary base and resulting in inflation. If central banks are independent, they can say no to such policies, at the same time being able to influence the economy to stabilize it.

But there was a solution: finance the deficits in the financial market by issuing bonds. In other words, politicians were still able to run deficits, but instead of asking their central banks to "print" money, they just started issuing bonds, increasing the national debt. This is Greece, Portugal and, on a smaller scale, Italy's case. Another form of economic populism was deregulating the economic system to permit people to borrow as much money as they wanted, giving them the feeling of being richer than they were in reality and boosting votes to incumbent parties. This was exactly Ireland and Latvia's case some years ago.

The main presupposition in both cases was that the financial market's rationality wouldn't let politicians go too far. However, as the financial market expectations were too optimistic, governments, and people in general, were able to borrow beyond anything rational. Thus, the crisis is, in its essence, the result of good old populism fueled by financial irrationality. Traditional political theory says that politicians will say anything voters want to get elected. It seems it's not like this anymore. Nowadays, politicians will say and do anything to please the financial markets, while lying to the voters that it's for their own good. Lies. It should be better to have Pinocchio as political leader. At least we'll know - his nose grows when he tells lies.

National Interest and Development: Some Remarks

Jan 11, 2012

There has been a lot of debate on the European crisis and the Eurozone's future. Some pundits wrote about the possibility of a European war, and Nicolas Sarkozy even compared a possible Eurozone failure with the end of the world as we know it. It is not a surprise that, even with competent economists, we still have problems with basic economic policy. Paraphrasing one of Bill Clinton's campaign mottos, "it's the politicians, stupid."

The fact is that the economic system's behavior is determined at the political level, as nowadays there is no real economic liberalism. Instead, the system is highly regulated to assure it is fair for everyone (or at least it should be).In other words, the markets are not that free to do what they want. They have to follow the rules created by politicians and technocrats. Thus, the root of the crisis is to be found at the political level: it's all because of the neoliberal version of the good old economic populism, this time boosted by the financial markets and the lack of a credible economic and political alternative to Neo-liberalism.

It all started with the establishment of the nation-state. Each country, besides being political institutions, is also recognized as an economic entity. Thus, the concept of political economy in the very beginning was already established the rivalry of nation-states looking for the best way to become wealthier. One of the best examples is Adam Smith's "Wealth of Nations," whose principles British policy-makers applied very effectively when establishing and developing Great Britain's colonial empire.

This has been passed over to wanna-be developing states, making the ideology of development be connected to the notion of national identity. This explains why extreme right-wing regimes in Latin America, like Brazil, Argentina, and Chile (in a more moderate way) implemented policies of development based on each of these countries' national interests, called "national-developmentalism." It's not the case here to defend these policies or not, but the fact is that from basic commodities' (mostly coffee and sugar) exports until the 1930's, Brazil has overtaken Britain as the world's sixth largest economy in 2011. But what does this issue of national interest has to do with Europe's economic crisis? A lot.

The European Union is a mix of well-developed countries such as Germany and Sweden, with wanna-be developed countries like Portugal and Greece, and third-world countries like Bulgaria and Romania. One of the most important bases of the European pact is that the national interest should give way to the common interest of the union. However, it is not that simple. Although Brussels and its technocrats have a lot of influence in what happens within the European Union, in the last instance, it is the national governments that have the legitimation to decide on important political and economic issues. It is easy to find out that it is not the European Commission that is leading the discussions on the European crisis, but Angela Merkel and Nicolas Sarkozy, representing, respectively, German and French interests, while David Cameron clearly defends British interests.

The first issue is that politicians are elected locally. Thus, they are loyal to the people and corporations that are financing their campaigns and, on a lesser scale, to their voters. Thus, although politicians use the rhetoric of a united Europe, etc., what they really care about is their own country.

Germany has been pursuing clear policies of economic development based on increasing the productivity of the real economy. It has understood that first, the level of productivity in an economy depends on innovation and not on the amount of available wealth to its citizens, and second that, if the financial market is let alone, it will allocate resources badly in terms of economic development. Latvia is one of the best examples. Germany's economic system has been called "ordoliberal," where the state intervenes in the economy to assure that the free market will reach its full theoretical potential. These policies work and... surprise: among others, von Hayek can be considered an ordoliberal.

As a result of the difference in productivity between Germany and the rest of Europe, the Eurozone's problems will continue in 2012. The solution for the crisis chosen by Merkel and Sarkozy aims to produce a recession forcing costs - mostly for labor - to drop, with the objective of indirectly increasing productivity. At the same time, Germany will continue to develop, increasing the structural gap with other EU countries even more. It's a matter of national interests. It's time for us in Latvia to learn From Germany.

Friedman, Schwartz, Keynes and the Eurozone

Feb 15, 2012

The economic debate in Brazil is well developed, with a very high level of theoretical sophistication. This is easily explained by the fact that Brazilian economists still have to read Adam Smith, David Ricardo, Stuart Mill, Jevons, Marshall, Keynes, and Kalecki, among others, as part of their intellectual formation. The idea is simple: knowing the great masters makes you to construct more robust models, and at the same time it impedes snake-oil salesmen from fooling around. The European Union and Latvia are full of them.

Discussing the Eurozone's problems with a Brazilian friend, who is also an economist, we remembered the interviews that two brilliant monetarists, Milton Friedman and Anna Schwartz, authors of the classic "A Monetary History of the United States: 1867-1960", gave to The Region, the Federal Reserve Bank of Minneapolis' magazine, in June of 1992 and September of 1993.

Answering the question "What are your thoughts on

89

Europe's plan for one currency?", Friedman answered that "I believe it will not come to an achievement in my lifetime. It may in yours, but I'm not sure that's true either." He also added that "it would be highly desirable if Europe could have a common money, a single unified money, just as it's desirable for the United States that we have a single unified currency. But in order for that to be possible or desirable, you have to have a unified currency over an area in which people and goods move relatively freely, and in which there is enough homogeneity of interest so that severe political strains are not raised by divergent developments in different parts of the area. If the Northeast were a separate country with a different language from the rest of the country, with a supposedly national government, it would be very tempted to resort to devaluation." Later, he also stated that "In order to have a truly unified currency. You need to have at most one true central bank, you have to eliminate the Bank of France, the Bank of Italy, the Deutsche Bundesbank, the Bank of England and so forth. The plans that are being made call for such a central bank, but it's a long cry from calling for it and having it."

Anna Schwartz answered a similar question in September 1993. The Region asked "does history have any lessons for the planners of a European monetary union?" Schwartz answered that the "planners of a European monetary union would be well advised to study the reasons the pre-World War I gold standard was a successful monetary regime, why the Genoa Economic Conference of

1922 and the London Economic Conference of 1933 failed, why the interwar gold standards collapsed, why Bretton Woods did not survive inflation in the center country (USA), and why the exchange rate mechanism has been on the ropes since 1992. The lessons of the past are that a monetary regime succeeds when countries with similar goals face similar shocks. Member countries have to be willing to yield national sovereignty to a supranational monetary authority. In an uncertain world subject to unforeseen and unanticipated shocks, countries have national priorities that do not preclude the use of domestic monetary policy and are reluctant to commit themselves to a common goal like price stability. The history of international monetary regimes suggests that a European monetary union is a nonstarter."

Schwartz and Friedman's point is simple: in the Eurozone, the Euro fixes each country exchange rate nominally. However, each country's real exchange rate floats virtually as a result of individual economic dynamics. The same applies for Latvia. Between 2004 and 2008 the currency was overvalued by more than 20% in relation to the Euro because of the difference of inflation rates experienced in Latvia and in the Eurozone. In real federations this is solved by the central government, which redistributes resources to regions with virtual deficits in their current accounts.

Keynes presented a solution for the problem in his 1931's "An Economic Analysis of Unemployment" in the form of fiscal devaluation. The idea was that an ad valorem tariff on all imports plus a subsidy of the same amount on all exports would have the same effect as an exchange rate devaluation. The NBER has a paper ("Fiscal Devaluation", Working Paper 17.662, December 2011) where the authors discuss the effects of fiscal devaluation using the New-Keynesian Dynamic Stochastic General Equilibrium model. It's a pity that European politicians are trying to forbid Keynesianism in Europe. Instead, they should learn from the great masters. Ah, they don't have time. I forgot.

Hayek, Economic Cycles, and the EU

Mar 21, 2012

I am known for criticizing both the Austrian School of economics and Milton Friedman's monetarist school. To make a long discussion short, although they have their degree of truth, as do all theories, they are based on flawed presuppositions - including those regarding human nature, and the role of government. Nevertheless, because of a discussion about Liaquat Ahamed's excellent book "Lords of Finance: the Bankers who Broke the World," I had to come back to Friedrich von Hayek's "Monetary Theory and the Trade Cycle," originally published in 1929. Although there are some minor problems regarding issues about the neutrality of money, Hayek's analysis is very astute.

He believed that bank credit is the ultimate cause of cycles; he gave more importance to its impact on the productive structure. His theory combines a Wicksellian theoretical base with the process of increasing and decreasing the production of capital goods relative to consumer goods. Two fundamental elements of his analysis are: (a) the idea of domestic economic equilibrium resulting from the equality of domestic savings and investment, and

(b) the disruption of this equilibrium is caused by monetary/credit disturbances, rather than price disturbances.

The cycle starts following a credit expansion resulting from the accumulation of loanable funds, making the natural rate of interest fall below the real interest rate, i.e. the interest rate resulting in equilibrium. An investment expansion follows, increasing the demand for capital goods, thus making the aggregate demand greater than the aggregate supply. However, as loans are used to increase the production of capital goods, there is a momentary relative shortage of consumer goods resulting in rising prices and in forced savings, funding a further expansion of credit. As the rising prices of consumer goods increase sectorial profits, their production also expands, pressuring the capital goods sector. In this moment, the production of both consumer and capital goods can even increase together.

This process will take place until full-employment is reached. In this case, the rising demand for consumer goods will result in rising prices again. This will make the consumer goods' sector more profitable than the capital-goods' sector, making both sectors compete for factors of production. This process will result in rising factor-costs, i.e. wages and interest rates. As the capital goods' sector dynamics are structurally fragile, higher wages resulting in decreasing profits, and higher interest rates reducing the overall investment level, decrease the demand for its products. As a consequence of the natural contraction process, people are fired, first in the capital goods' sector. As these people stop consuming, the consumer goods' sector also shrinks, making the investment level fall further, as consumer goods' firms also demand capital goods. The production of capital goods falls again, etc. Thus, the business cycle is inherent to a credit economy.

Accordingly to Hayek, the divergence between the natural and real interest rate is a natural output of the process of economic development. It represents a tendency in the economic system. It is endogenous to the system. Although the disturbance may not be monetary, money is what gets in the way of an immediate adjustment to a new equilibrium. In this sense, monetary creation is the most sensitive issue. Although changes in the money supply may result from flows of capital and issuance of central banks, the most important issue is the often disputed creation of deposits by private banks. That's why Hayek defended the idea that the financial sector must be regulated.

After WWII, the third event of catastrophic proportions in 70 years, European states started to understand that instead of retaliation, it was better to construct a common Europe. The main supporters of this idea, Jean Monet, Konrad Adenauer, and Alcide de Gaspari, articulated a European Union following the notion already present in

Adam Smith's Wealth of Nations, that trade and common economic interests can substitute for conflict and war.

With the end of the dollar-gold standard in 1971, banks became able to create as much fiat money as they wished, mostly as a result of increasing credit and derivatives. The financial system's greed for profits, even if based on fictional money, is making the economic system very unstable. At the limit, it is also responsible for the problems in Greece, Portugal, Italy, Ireland, and Spain. It was the financial system's lack of rationality that made it possible for populist politicians to make public debt go into the stratosphere. Hayek was right, and the concrete result is the current crisis.

Politicians have been unable to seriously discuss policies for regulating the financial system and to limit derivatives. They should. An unstable economic system results in unstable politics. Financial irrationality combined with political stupidity is harming the 20th century's most civilizatory political experience.

Time to be Bolder

Apr 26, 2012

Latvia's Minister of Economics Daniels Pavluts published an article (Nacionālā industriālā politika – 'ekonomikas izraviena' pamāts) on April 23 discussing the National Plan of Development (NAP). His main question was "what is most important regarding Latvia's development in the next five or ten years?

I have to confess I was positively surprised to read some of his opinions. First, and most significant, is that we are not as developed as many politicians and academic personnel claimed some years ago. I still can remember some people saying Latvia was almost as developed as the USA. Narcotics? No. Just exacerbated optimism and a lack of self-criticism. To recognize we need to develop is the first step to really starting to cope with our problems in a pragmatic way.

Second, he recognizes that industrialized countries like Germany were less affected by the crisis than the ones basing their economy on financial illusions like Latvia and the PIIGS. Also a very important step to make Latvia's macro-economy is to focus on promoting development instead of merely pleasing the financial sector. Third, that we are responsible for our development, meaning that we need an effective industrial policy. Finally, it was an adult text written by a Latvian Minister of Economics, although sometimes too optimistic and quite propagandistic. That's why I would like this article not to be considered a criticism, but rather an exchange of viewpoints.

It is true that Latvia's GDP has grown 5.5 percent in real terms last year. However, this is, first, the result of what can be considered a natural rebound of the Latvian economy. People became too cautious. Second, it reflects the internal devaluation's effects on the economy. Taking in consideration the export value unit index (data from Latvijas Statistika), the recent recession reduced our international prices around by 20.5 percent between 2007, the peak, and 2009. The result was the export boom of the last two years, with exports growing 61.1 percent in real terms between 2009 and 2011. The conclusion is simple: whatever was internal or not, devaluation boosts exports.

Nevertheless, there is no motive to believe exports will continue to grow so smoothly. First, unfortunately, between 2009 and 2011 Latvia's export value unit index increased almost 25 percent, practically reaching 2007 levels. In other words, the effects of the internal devaluation are over. Add a growing GDP and the result is that, after experiencing a decrease in its deficit between

2007 and 2010 (and even a surplus in 2009 and 2010), Latvia's current account was again deficitary in 2011. The same applies to 2012's first two months. If it is to expect that our exports will stabilize at the current level, it is also to expect that the GDP will not grow at the same magnitude as last year.

This also explains the prognosis that Latvia's GDP will grow between 2 percent and 3 percent this year. In fact, taking in consideration that Latvia is relatively under-developed, a growth of this magnitude is extremely mediocre. Of course, in Germany's case, it could be considered a very good performance, but even Argentina's GDP has been growing around 8 percent per year since 2003. That is why Mr. Pavluts is convinced that Latvia needs a solid industrial policy to provide support to business based on clever and modern analysis. But what is an industrial policy based on clever and modern analysis?

Some months ago there was a debate about policies for development, led by LTV1 journalist Egils Zarins, in which experts discussed policies for development. After some time, two groups naturally formed. One led by Mr. Pavluts and Vjaceslavs Dombrovskis; the other by Janis Oslejs and Sergejs Ancupovs. The first defended basically a more pragmatic version of good ol' Neo-liberalism, while the second supported the idea we have to learn from South Korea and Finland.

Based on what was said there, Mr. Pavluts' industrial policy, based on clever and modern analysis, is the one that, in privatizing Lattelecom, Latvenergo, LMT, among others, increasing the efficiency of institutions, supporting the establishment of small and micro enterprises, as of innovation as well, and at the same time determining which are Latvia's strategic sectors, results in development.

With the exception of privatizing profitable infrastructure companies, I agree that these ideas are good and necessary. The problem is that there is no proven direct causal relation between them and economic development. They are necessary, but not sufficient.

Latvia's economic policies are based on many urban legends, like "adopting the euro will result in investment," just to cite the most common one. If we are to develop, we need to go beyond conventionalism and hoaxes. Nowadays, this sadly means to learn with History.

Scorpions, Unemployment and Development

Oct 03, 2012

There is a well-known fable in which a scorpion asks a frog to carry him across a river. Although the frog is afraid of being stung during the journey, the scorpion convinces it otherwise, saying that if the frog sinks, the scorpion would drown too. The frog agrees, but, in the middle of the river, the scorpion stings the frog. The frog asks why and the scorpion just answers: "This is my nature." The fable has many variations, substituting the frog with a turtle or the scorpion with a snake. In the end, it's about the fact that many times nature determines behavior, notwithstanding the consequences.

Putting this fable into perspective with the current global crisis, the unregulated financial sector killed the real sector, while politicians and the government were applauding and some economists were constructing mathematical models to explain and support what was happening. Taking into consideration that any economic policy implemented by politicians is based on economic models developed by the academia, are economists guilty of the crisis? The answer is: partially. For sure they helped to establish an ideology giving pseudo-scientific support to the idea that an unregulated financial sector would boost development and welfare, and politicians avidly bought this idea.

The idea is that markets are perfect and government is always bad. Based on this presupposition, economists did academic work inventing parallel universes, where societies produce only one product, where the aggregate production function is constant, one agent represents all consumers and producers, and there are neither credit nor stock markets. Sounds unrealistic, isn't it? Economists know it is. That's why economists can now argue that the politicians are guilty. After all, they believed in and misused models that were about imaginary worlds. On the other hand, bad choices for economic policy leading to unemployment results in bad performance in elections. Latvia's People's Party is a good example. And then politicians can also argue: "But we trusted you! You fooled us with your unreal models."

A good example of this pattern is the IMF Working Paper 12/189, E. B. Yehoue's "On Price Stability and Welfare." He concludes that using "a conservative representative-agent general equilibrium model, and based on parameter values that are consistent with U.S. data, the paper estimates welfare costs associated with various levels of inflation targets, in particular, 2, 4, and 10 percent. The findings suggest that the additional welfare costs of raising inflation targets from 2 to 4 percent are equal to about 0.3 percent of real income. For a rise from 2 to 10 percent, the additional welfare costs are estimated at about 1 percent of real income. Finally, the use of other values for the constant parameter in the money demand curves yield estimates as high as 7 percent of real income for raising the inflation target from 2 to 4 percent, and 30 percent of real income for raising the target from 2 to10 percent." (p. 4).

As a good econometrist, the rule is "give the numbers and I'll prove anything you want." In the paper's 35 pages, only once (p. 21) does the word unemployment appear, and none of the 58 reference titles mention unemployment. This is the economic ideology that has been guiding Latvia's economic policy until now. Losing around 6.5 percent of its population due to migration since 2008, Latvia is a victim of this ideology.

The government was right to not pursue populist measures like permitting uncontrolled budget deficits and devaluation. Because of the lack of a pragmatic plan of development and industrial policy, that would only make things worse. In this sense, the chosen policies were correct to deal with the crisis and getting rid of the IMF. However, a crucial mistake was assuming that austerity and internal devaluation would result in strong development. They don't, as the effects of internal devaluation are already gone.

That's why it's good news that now there is a development plan. Although it has been very much criticized, it's the first time Latvia has such a plan with concrete measures to promote development and employment, instead of just repeating "we will be the most competitive nation in 20 years," hoping that some miracle will happen.

The plan is not perfect. Still there's a lot to do and discuss, but at least it seems that the government finally understood that a sound financial sector is only part of the equation for development. Much more needed is the correct set of incentives to let the private sector develop in a way that will result in employment, higher productivity and higher wages. Hopefully this will stop migration and will make Latvians abroad come back to Latvia.

www.ingramcontent.com/pod-product-compliance
Lightning Source LLC
Chambersburg PA
CBHW071521200326
41519CB00019B/6022